FREDERICKSBURG NATIONAL CEMETERY, Fredericksburg, Virginia

PROFESSOR THADDEUS S. C. LOWE, balloon observer
and Union chief of army aeronautics, Fair Oaks, Virginia, 1862

Published by Thomasson-Grant, Inc.
Designed by Leonard G. Phillips
Edited by Hoke Perkins

Color separations by Pioneer Graphic through CGI (Malaysia) Sdn. Bhd.
Printed and bound in Singapore by Eurasia Press (Offset), Pte. Ltd.
We wish to acknowledge the many pilots whose cooperation and skill
made this book possible, especially Caleb and Mervin Glick of Waynesboro, Virginia.
Special thanks go to Jimmy Heidel, director of the Vicksburg Chamber of Commerce,
and to the Mississippi Power and Light Company.

97 96 95 94 93 92 91 90   5 4 3 2 1

Library of Congress Cataloging-in-Publication Data
Abell, Sam
The Civil War.
1. United States—History—Civil War, 1861-1865—
Aerial photographs. I. Pohanka, Brian C., 1955-
II. Title.
E468.7.A23 1990 779′.99737 89-20467
ISBN 0-934738-61-0

Thomasson-Grant
One Morton Drive, Suite 500
Charlottesville, Virginia 22901
(804) 977-1780

THE CIVIL WAR
AN AERIAL PORTRAIT

PHOTOGRAPHY BY SAM ABELL

TEXT BY BRIAN POHANKA

THOMASSON-GRANT
Charlottesville, Virginia

NEW YORK PEACE MONUMENT, Lookout Mountain, Chickamauga and Chattanooga National Military Park, Tennessee

AT THE HEIGHT OF THE BATTLE OF FRANKLIN, as Union troops entrenched around the little Tennessee town struggled to repel a massive Confederate assault, the men of the 65th Illinois caught glimpses through the battle smoke of a mounted Confederate officer riding back and forth in front of the Rebel line. Miraculously unscathed in the crossfire, he was exhorting his troops to attack the Union earthworks.

Suddenly the horseman galloped headlong out of the smoke toward the Union line, leaping the ditch and gaining the crest of the rampart before the defenders could react. Awed by this display of suicidal bravery and hoping to capture the officer alive, the commander of the 65th shouted at his men to hold their fire. But when the Rebel made a grab for the regiment's colors, dozens of Union bullets struck horse and rider down.

The Confederates fell back; the firing subsided. Crowding around the stricken Rebel, the Federals eased him from the saddle and gave him water from a canteen. An Indiana soldier snatched up a handful of cotton from a nearby gin and made a pillow for the officer's head. The Southerner thanked his enemies for their kindness and, when told that his wounds were mortal, gasped, "It is the fate of a soldier to die for his country."

The man whose courage had just cost him his life was 39-year-old Brigadier General John Adams of Tennessee, a graduate of West Point, veteran of the Mexican War, and former captain of United States Dragoons. Like many Southern-born career officers, he resigned his commission in 1861 and gave his allegiance to the Confederacy. By 1863, he attained general's rank, commanding a brigade of Mississippians which he led until his death at Franklin on November 30, 1864.

Adams's bravery was not unusual for a high-ranking officer in the Civil War; he fought in an age which expected officers to incite their soldiers to valiant deeds by personal example. At Seven Pines, Union General Philip Kearny galloped through a hail of bullets, saber in hand, shouting, "Forward! You'll find lovely fighting along the whole line!" At Gettysburg, Federal Corps Commander Winfield Scott Hancock rode coolly through a Confederate barrage, prompting an officer to comment, "One felt safe when near him." Amid the carnage of the Wilderness, Robert E. Lee put himself in such peril that his soldiers chorused, "Lee to the rear! Lee to the rear!"

Such bravery exacted a terrible price. At the Battle of Franklin alone, five Confederate generals died; a sixth succumbed to his wounds soon after. By war's end, 47 Union and 77 Confederate generals had been killed in battle or died from wounds received in action. These stunning losses in the higher echelons reflect the shared training of the officer corps on each side. Roughly a third of all Union and Confederate generals, including many of the best, had been schooled at the United States Military Academy at West Point, and many gained their first campaign experience together in the Mexican War. Whichever side they chose in the Civil War, they brought similar tactics and ideas to their commands.

Despite this common background, one of the great facts of the Civil War was the superiority of Southern military leadership in the first two years of the conflict. There were many reasons for the strength of the Southern officer class. Confederate President Jefferson Davis was himself a West Pointer, a successful field commander in the Mexican War, and secretary of war under President Franklin Pierce. Unlike Abraham Lincoln, Davis rarely allowed politics to dictate his selection of military commanders. The South's established military tradition made the pursuit of an army career far more fashionable there than in the North. Schools like the Virginia Military Institute and The Citadel offered an education virtually on a par with that provided by West Point. Perhaps most important, the fledgling nation faced an immediate threat to its survival that mandated recognition of military talent.

The North, on the other hand, was saddled with the existing military structure, a hierarchy founded upon seniority rather than ability. Moreover, political patronage was a fact of life for the Lincoln administration, and Lincoln had to allow politics to play a potent and frequently harmful role in the appointment of field commanders. Only with the cooperation of the governors of the Northern states could the Union's superiority in industry, transport, and manpower be decisively employed, and the price for the cooperation of the "war governors" was often the promotion of a political crony to a rank he was not qualified to hold. Nonetheless, as the war dragged on, the balance of military leadership shifted to the North. The wartime experiences of two young West Pointers tell the story of that shift.

IN THE EARLY DAYS OF 1861, as the likelihood of war increased, cadets at the Academy faced a choice: to remain, graduate, and assume their place in the regular army, or to resign and join the Confederacy. Thomas Lafayette Rosser and Emory Upton, two members of the class due to graduate in May, chose opposing sides and embarked on careers that would span four years of war and see them both achieve the rank of general officer.

Rosser and Upton were opposites in almost every way. Perhaps the only thing they had in common was the ambition to succeed in a military career. Rosser was born in 1836 on a farm in Campbell County, Virginia. When Tom was 12, his father moved the family to Panola County, Texas, where they raised cotton and corn on the banks of the Sabine River. The young Rosser grew into a rugged, boisterous outdoorsman, infinitely fonder of hunting and riding than of studying. Upon his arrival at West Point in the summer of

WEST POINT CADET EMORY UPTON, 1861

1856, the 6'2" Texan was described by a classmate as "a great, swarthy-looking cadet, who seemed altogether too big for his bobtailed coat and turned-over white collar."

Short and lean almost to emaciation, freckle-faced Emory Upton was three years younger than Rosser, and while he too was born into a farming family, his upbringing in Genesee County, New York, greatly differed from the garrulous Texan's. Quiet, intense, and deeply religious, Upton was a temperance advocate and an abolitionist. Before entering West Point, he had attended Oberlin College, a coeducational and racially integrated school in Ohio that supplied John Brown with several of his followers in the raid on Harpers Ferry. Upton's fervent antislavery views set him apart from many of his fellow cadets and brought on an inconclusive but bloody fistfight with an aristocratic young South Carolinian, Wade Hampton Gibbes. In later years, another classmate remembered the incident as "the most thrilling event" of their time at the Academy, one that "represented the issue between the States, and duly the courage and bitterness with which it was fought out to the end."

Rosser was not averse to fighting either; a brawl in the autumn of 1857 during which he drew his sword on a cadet captain from Massachusetts put him in solitary confinement for "conduct prejudicial to good order and military discipline." Like his good friend George Custer, Rosser racked up an impressive number of demerits during his tenure at West Point, and, like Custer, he proved something less than academically proficient, habitually ranking in the lowest fifth of his class. Upton, on the other hand, was a good student, a voracious reader of tactical manuals and military history. "His constant thought was about organization, tactics, strategy and logistics," a fellow West Pointer recalled. "He was a genuine military enthusiast, whose thoughts night and day turned to the art of War."

Upton was also an astute observer of the growing national crisis and the prospects for civil war. "Southern men are brave, and will fight well," he wrote in January 1861, "but their means for prosecuting a long war are wanting." As more and more Southern cadets resigned prior to graduation, Upton deplored the loss of energetic young men such as Rosser and the Alabamian John Pelham, who would soon become one of the Confederacy's great artillery commanders. He recognized that even before the first shots were fired, Jefferson Davis was "drawing all the talent he can from our army."

Rosser, who began his career as an artillery officer at First Manassas, served much of the war with the symbolic heart of the Southern cause, the Army of Northern Virginia. Under the leadership of Robert E. Lee, that army, more than any other Confederate command, managed to frustrate Northern efforts to wear the South down by weight of numbers and matériel. Following the Seven Days' Campaign in the early summer

WEST POINT CADET THOMAS LAFAYETTE ROSSER, 1858

of 1862, Lee implemented a crucial reorganization, replacing slow, incompetent, and uncooperative subordinates with energetic leaders who forged the Army of Northern Virginia into a seemingly unbeatable force. Success bred confidence and esprit de corps which, coupled with Lee's penchant for the strategic gamble, enabled Confederate forces in the eastern theater to outfight a succession of Northern opponents.

Rosser rose swiftly through the ranks, becoming colonel of the 5th Virginia Cavalry in June 1862, and was soon regarded as one of the most dashing protégés of that quintessentially dashing horse soldier, General James Ewell Brown Stuart. Not only did Rosser look the part of the cavalier in his gold-embroidered frock coat and plumed hat, he exemplified the fighting spirit that in the first two years of the war enabled the Confederate cavalry to consistently defeat their plodding Federal counterparts. Jeb Stuart took note of Rosser's "extraordinary merit, unsurpassed ability, and conspicuous gallantry," stating, "no officer I have met with in the Confederacy combines in a more eminent degree the characteristics of the Cavalry commander."

By 1863, Rosser's bravery had brought him two wounds and innumerable accolades. His wartime wedding to a Virginia belle attracted "the flower of the Confederate service," while his battlefield prowess won him promotion to brigadier general and command of a brigade of Virginia cavalry. In one daring assault, Rosser ordered his outmanned troopers to attack a superior Federal force from the front, flank, and rear. After this imaginative action, part of a cavalry campaign against Federal supply bases in West Virginia, Jeb Stuart declared that Rosser had "added fresh laurels" to his unit's already distinguished record. Soon Rosser's men were sporting sprigs of laurel in their caps and calling themselves the "Laurel Brigade."

While Rosser threw himself into battle with swashbuckling bravado, Upton began his career by attending rigorously to tactics. When he assumed command of the 121st New York in the autumn of 1862, he required his officers to memorize every page of army regulations and tactical manuals and imposed strict discipline on the men in the ranks. He had, one of his men recalled, "the appearance of a man who was deeply impressed with the seriousness of warfare."

In combat, the young colonel coupled fearless and inspirational leadership with an ability to take in the tactical situation at a glance. His superiors in the 6th Corps rewarded him with elevation to brigade command, but the star of a brigadier general was at first denied him. Although extremely talented, Upton lacked political influence, the most important ingredient for promotion in the Union army. Like many other Northern veterans, Upton fumed at his government's inability to properly mobilize and coordinate the war

FORT PULASKI NATIONAL MONUMENT, Cockspur Island, Georgia

effort. "We have got men enough," he wrote, "and have only to bring them out." He expressed disdain for senior officers who lacked fighting spirit, declaring, "Some of our Corps commanders are not fit to be corporals."

Upton's frustration was shared by his commander in chief, Abraham Lincoln. Despite his relative inexperience in military matters, Lincoln grew to be a masterful judge of ability, but was unable to find a general who could bring Lee's army to bay. The most promising Northern commander in the first two years of the conflict, Major General George B. McClellan, ultimately proved to be one of the most disappointing. Intelligent, charismatic, and a brilliant organizer, McClellan imbued his Army of the Potomac with such confidence that he was dubbed "the Young Napoleon." Yet McClellan lacked the Napoleonic virtue Lee possessed in abundance: the willingness to take risks. "There is only one safe rule in war," McClellan once wrote, "to decide what is the very worst thing that can happen to you and prepare to meet it." Lincoln eventually found Ulysses S. Grant, of course, a general eminently possessed of the aggressive instinct McClellan lacked. Under Grant's direction, the eastern armies moved relentlessly closer to Richmond, while the equally relentless William Tecumseh Sherman carved a path through Georgia and South Carolina. Thoroughly indifferent to the customary pageantry of 19th-century soldiering and eager to bring the murderous conflict to a swift end, Grant and Sherman took the art of war a step closer to the modern age. They cut loose from bases of supply, confiscated the produce and livestock of the civilian population, and destroyed what could not be consumed.

In this climate, talented young officers like Emory Upton began to thrive. Attrition and plain military necessity had at last weeded out most of the political appointees, foreign adventurers, and military incompetents among Grant's and Sherman's subordinates. By 1864, a new generation of Federal officers formed the backbone of the Union army, enabling the North not merely to overwhelm the South with numbers, but to master Confederate forces with battlefield tactics.

When Grant came east in the spring of 1864, the war in Virginia entered its last and deadliest phase. Forced to go on the defensive, Lee's troops fought from the cover of earthen and log breastworks. The Yankees entrenched in turn. While many Federal officers despaired at the heavy losses the new trench warfare entailed, Upton was convinced that the proper tactical methods would carry even the strongest fortifications. On May 10, 1864, the fourth day of the Spotsylvania Campaign, he got the chance to put his theories into practice.

Placed in command of 12 handpicked regiments, Upton planned and executed a

CONFEDERATE ARTILLERY POSITION, Gettysburg National Military Park, Pennsylvania

daring assault on the western flank of a heavily defended salient called the Mule Shoe. He deployed the troops in four lines that advanced rapidly in successive waves, avoiding crowding and excessive casualties. There was no pause to fire; too often in the past, the gradual advance of a firing line had sacrificed the element of surprise Upton considered crucial to success. Upton's plan worked. The men, relying on their momentum and their fixed bayonets, broke through the Confederate position. Once within the works, the leading ranks divided, swinging to the left and right, enlarging the breach and taking some 1,200 prisoners in the process. The attack might have proved decisive had Upton's forces been properly supported. As it was, the Confederates rallied and plugged the gap in their line. But Upton's ingenious assault won him the promotion to general he had long deserved.

Grant's inexorable advance in Virginia began to wear down Lee's army, and the changing tide of war severely affected the Confederate cavalry, for in numbers, armament, and leadership the Northern troopers had at last surpassed their once-invincible Southern foes. Tom Rosser confessed to his wife, "The Yankee cavalry can manage our cavalry so easily that they can ride over our country whenever they choose." The death of Jeb Stuart in May 1864 dampened the spirits of the Confederate horsemen, and Rosser did not get on well with Stuart's successor, Wade Hampton. Nevertheless, Rosser continued to fight with characteristic zeal; in the clash at Todd's Tavern his brigade bested a Federal division, Rosser charging at the head of the column, saber in hand, as a major galloped alongside shouting, "General, isn't this glorious!" At Trevilian Station on June 11, 1864, while engaging a force that included his old friend George Custer, Rosser took a bullet in the knee that put him out of action for two months. Not long after his return, Rosser received welcome orders transferring the Laurel Brigade to a new theater of war, the Shenandoah Valley.

Upton had preceded Rosser to the Valley. In the late summer of 1864, the 6th Corps joined the army of Philip Sheridan, who soon embarked on a ruthless and ultimately victorious campaign to wrest control of the "breadbasket of the Confederacy" from Jubal A. Early's army. On September 19, Upton played a conspicuous part in Sheridan's defeat of Early at Winchester. Taking command of the division when his superior officer was killed, Upton was struck by a shell fragment that ripped open his thigh and exposed the femoral artery. After a tourniquet was applied, Upton ordered four soldiers to carry him along the battle line in a stretcher. In his memoirs, General James H. Wilson, commander of a cavalry division in Sheridan's army, called Upton's conduct "the most heroic action that came under my observation during the war."

The arrival of the dashing Rosser and his veteran troopers seemed promising

STATE CAPITOL, Richmond, Virginia

to Early's battered forces. Rosser was soon being called "the Savior of the Valley," a sobriquet he did nothing to discourage, and was rewarded with command of a division on October 5. The day after taking charge, Rosser accepted the challenge offered by the Union cavalry and gave battle at Tom's Brook. Spotting Custer at the head of a division of blueclad horsemen, Rosser exchanged salutes before charging into the fray. Unfortunately for the Confederate commander, the élan which had won so many victories in the past was now futile. Outnumbered, outgunned, outflanked, the Confederate force was routed in what one brigade commander called "the greatest disaster that ever befell our cavalry." In the wake of the defeat, the acerbic Early commented, "I say, Rosser, your brigade had better take the grape leaf for a badge. The laurel is a running vine."

For Rosser, the last months of the war were bitter ones, as bravery and endurance were of no avail in retrieving the waning fortunes of the Confederacy. He was in the thick of the action until the end, snatching what glory he could from the worsening strategic situation. When the Union stranglehold tightened on Lee's army at Appomattox on April 9, 1865, and surrender became a certainty, Rosser and several hundred cavalrymen managed to cut their way through the Yankee lines. In later years, Rosser called the exploit the "greatest triumph of my military career, indeed I may say of my life." But his defiance proved fruitless, and a month later, he too surrendered.

Upton, who had begun his career as an artilleryman and spent two years leading infantry, finished the war commanding a cavalry division in General Wilson's massive raid through Alabama and Georgia in the spring of 1865. This campaign provided Upton the perfect opportunity to pursue his tactical theories and versatile approach to warfare. No longer was the cavalry the worst-organized and least-confident branch of the service; they were shock troops, armed with rapid-firing Spencer carbines that made them equally effective mounted or on foot. Storming the Confederate fortifications that ringed Selma, Alabama, Upton's division proved that dismounted cavalry could function as infantry not only on the skirmish line, but in a successful assault on Confederate earthworks. His brilliant wartime service, characterized by courage and tactical genius, won Upton promotion to the rank of brevet major general.

After the war, the classmates once more chose separate paths. Rosser left the military and prospered as a civil engineer on the western frontier and as a Republican politician in his native Virginia. In 1898, he donned a blue uniform and trained troops for the Spanish-American War. When he died in 1910, Rosser was eulogized as an exemplar of national reconciliation.

Upton spent the rest of his life in the army. Following the loss of his young wife

BURNSIDE'S BRIDGE, Antietam National Battlefield, Maryland

to tuberculosis in 1870, he devoted all of his time to military research and theory. He was appointed commandant of cadets at West Point, visited the armies of Europe and Asia, and was assigned the task of revising the United States Army's tactics. In his new system, set forth in three books on infantry, cavalry, and artillery maneuvers, Upton brought American tactics out of the Napoleonic and into the modern age, emphasizing the lessons learned at such human cost in four years of civil war. He has been called one of three military theorists (along with Jomini and Clausewitz) who "shaped, and continue to shape, the way Americans look at war."

Equally mindful of the mismanagement of Union armies on the strategic level, Upton prepared a revolutionary evaluation of American military policy. He finished this landmark work in 1880, but did not live to see its publication in 1904. In the end, Upton, who had survived the hazards of serving as a general in America's bloodiest war, became a casualty of overwork, depression, and tormenting headaches. On March 15, 1881, he committed suicide at his quarters in San Francisco's Presidio.

"OUR MEN HAVE, IN MANY INSTANCES, been foolishly and wantonly sacrificed," Upton wrote in June of 1864. "Thousands of lives might have been spared by the exercise of a little skill." This was an opinion he never revised. In 1879, Upton branded the system that had governed the wartime armies "a crime against life, a crime against property, and a crime against liberty." The more "modern" generals held much the same view; Sherman wrote that American commanders were prone to the "cruel and inhuman act" of sending undisciplined forces against superior troops, exposing them to certain defeat. It is one of the tragedies of the American Civil War that few Union or Confederate officers agreed with Upton. Like Tom Rosser, like John Adams, they relied on patriotic zeal, inspirational leadership, and personal bravery to carry the day, using antiquated tactics that condemned thousands of them to heroic but wasteful deaths.

Brian C. Pohanka
Alexandria, Virginia

ILLINOIS MONUMENT, Missionary Ridge, Chickamauga and Chattanooga National Military Park, Tennessee

KELLY'S FORD, Rappahannock River, Virginia

*A*nd I saw askant the armies,

    I saw as in noiseless dreams hundreds of battle-flags,

    Borne through the smoke of the battles and pierc'd with missiles I saw them,

    And carried hither and yon through the smoke, and torn and bloody,

    And at last but a few shreds left on the staffs, (and all in silence,)

    And the staffs all splinter'd and broken.

Walt Whitman
from ''When Lilacs Last in the Dooryard Bloom'd''

FORT JEFFERSON NATIONAL MONUMENT, Garden Key, Florida. When the Civil War
began in the spring of 1861, both sides moved quickly to gain control of coastal fortifications
originally designed to protect the United States from foreign invasion. Seventy miles beyond
Key West in the Gulf of Mexico, Fort Jefferson remained in Union hands throughout the conflict,
serving as a military prison.

FORT SUMTER NATIONAL MONUMENT, South Carolina. Shortly before dawn on April 12, 1861, Confederate batteries ringing Charleston Harbor opened fire on Fort Sumter, an outpost defended by 128 men under the command of Major Robert Anderson. Isolated and outgunned, the garrison surrendered two days later to Confederate Brigadier General P. G. T. Beauregard. Beauregard, who had served as superintendent of West Point, resigned his commission when his native state, Louisiana, seceded from the Union.

STONE HOUSE AND HENRY HOUSE, Manassas National Battlefield Park, Virginia

*E*very segment of line we succeeded in forming was again dissolved while another was being formed; more than two thousand men were shouting each some suggestion to his neighbor, their voices mingling with the noise of the shells hurtling through the trees overhead, and all word of command drowned in the confusion and uproar. It was at this moment that General Bee used the famous expression, "Look at Jackson's brigade! It stands there like a stone wall"—a name that passed from the brigade to its immortal commander.

General P. G. T. Beauregard, C.S.A.
First Manassas

COMPANY DRILL, 2nd Rhode Island Infantry, near Washington, D.C., winter 1861-62. On July 21, 1861, Brigadier General Irvin McDowell's inexperienced Union army attacked Beauregard's equally novice force along Bull Run, a muddy stream in northern Virginia. The First Battle of Manassas was the brutal introduction to combat for dozens of hastily recruited volunteer regiments, including the 2nd Rhode Island. One of the first units to become engaged, the regiment lost 98 men in a matter of minutes. Their commanding officer, Colonel John S. Slocum, was shot through the head leading a charge.

HENRY HOUSE HILL, Manassas. At first, the battle went well for the North; three Southern brigades were forced to retreat to a hilltop crowned by Judith Henry's white frame house. The Federal infantry pursued, and the batteries of Captains James B. Ricketts and Charles Griffin unlimbered near the Henry House, preparing to blast a way through the wavering Confederate line. Then came the battle's decisive moment, as Confederate Brigadier General Thomas J. Jackson held his regiments in position, gaining time for the Rebels to regroup. When the blue-uniformed soldiers of the 33rd Virginia advanced on the Union artillery, they were mistaken for Federal troops. The Confederates poured a volley into the cannoneers at point-blank range and overran the position.

STONE BRIDGE, Manassas. Beauregard envisioned Bull Run as a natural moat between his army and McDowell's. For two hours, Union officers hesitated to launch an attack on the narrow stone bridge that carried the Warrenton Pike over the stream. Then Colonel William Tecumseh Sherman's brigade marched upstream, forded Bull Run, and flanked the Confederate defenders at the bridgehead. When Confederate reinforcements under Brigadier General Joseph E. Johnston turned the tide of battle four hours later, they pushed many of these same Union troops back across the bridge in a disheartened retreat toward Washington, 20 miles away.

ROBINSON HOUSE AND HENRY HOUSE HILL, Manassas. Some of the battle's heaviest fighting occurred on a farm owned by James Robinson, a free black. Early on, Confederate forces were driven with heavy losses across his fields to Henry House Hill. In late afternoon, Union troops retreated northward over the same ground. "The retreat soon became a rout," General McDowell reported, "and soon degenerated still further into a panic." The Confederates controlled the field at the end of the day, but confusion and chance marked both sides' maneuvers in the war's first great test of generalship.

BALL'S BLUFF, Virginia. On October 21, 1861, a Union expedition into Confederate-occupied Loudoun County, Virginia, met with disaster when 1,700 men scaled a 70-foot bluff on the Potomac River. The Federal commander, Colonel Edward D. Baker, had not properly scouted the Confederate positions; Virginians and Mississippians rushed the Yankee troops after they made the climb, forcing them over the edge of the bluff and into the Potomac. Hundreds drowned while attempting to swim to the safety of Harrison's Island (foreground). Baker, a close friend of Abraham Lincoln, was killed early in the battle.

WHITE'S FERRY AND HARRISON'S ISLAND, Potomac River. The fiasco at Ball's Bluff reinforced the characteristic caution of Major General George B. McClellan, who had assumed command of the Union armies in July 1861. But if McClellan preferred drilling and organizing his Army of the Potomac to campaigning, neither did his Confederate counterpart, Joseph E. Johnston, seek a major engagement. The war in the east became a waiting game, with Yankee and Rebel pickets exchanging frequent taunts and occasional shots across the river that divided them.

FORT DONELSON, Fort Donelson National Battlefield Park, Tennessee

General Smith began the advance.... He was, of course, a conspicuous object for the sharp-shooters in the rifle-pits. The air around him twittered with minie-bullets. Erect as if on review, he rode on, timing the gait of his horse with the movement of his colors.... Some of the men halted, whereupon, seeing the hesitation, General Smith put his cap on the point of his sword, held it aloft, and called out, "No flinching now, my lads!—Here—this is the way! Come on!" He picked a path through the jagged limbs of the trees, holding his cap all the time in sight; and the effect was magical. The men swarmed in after him.

General Lew Wallace, U.S.A.
on General Charles F. Smith, U.S.A.
Fort Donelson

I saw the men standing in knots talking in the most excited manner. No officer seemed to be giving any directions. The soldiers had their muskets, but no ammunition, while there were tons of it close at hand.... I directed Colonel Webster to ride with me and call out to the men as we passed: "Fill your cartridge boxes, quick, and get into line; the enemy is trying to escape and he must not be allowed to do so...." The men only wanted some one to give them a command.

General Ulysses S. Grant, U.S.A.
Fort Donelson

LIEUTENANT GENERAL ULYSSES SIMPSON GRANT, U.S.A., circa 1864. The meteoric rise of Grant, a soft-spoken, failed businessman and ex-regular army officer, began in February 1862 with his capture of Forts Henry and Donelson, vital Confederate posts on the Tennessee and Cumberland rivers. Control of the rivers provided the western armies with a natural avenue into the heart of the Confederacy. Grant's tactics at Fort Donelson revealed his greatest military asset: a dogged determination to win at any price.

NATIONAL CEMETERY, Fort Donelson. Pinned down in their fortifications, their backs to the Cumberland River (right), the Confederate defenders of Fort Donelson waged a losing four-day battle with Grant's besieging army. A breakout attempt was thwarted when Grant commanded Brigadier General Charles F. Smith to lead a risky counterattack on the fort. On February 16, 1862, after two days of fighting in snowstorms and subfreezing temperatures, Confederate Major General Simon Bolivar Buckner capitulated to Grant's demand for unconditional surrender. Although some 10,000 Southern troops laid down their arms, the Union, too, paid a price. The cemetery at the site holds 670 Federal soldiers, 512 of them buried as unknowns.

SHILOH BATTLEFIELD AND TENNESSEE RIVER, Shiloh National Military Park, Tennessee. After capturing the river forts, Grant marched into middle Tennessee, planning to join Major General Don Carlos Buell's forces for a major spring offensive into Mississippi. Confederate General Albert Sidney Johnston moved northeast from Corinth to confront Grant before he could rendezvous with Buell. In the early morning hours of Sunday, April 6, 1862, Johnston's 40,000 troops struck Grant's army camped between Shiloh Church and Pittsburg Landing on the Tennessee River. Caught completely by surprise, thousands of Yankees fled toward the river bluffs.

HORNET'S NEST, Shiloh. Johnston had assured his generals, "Tonight we will water our horses in the Tennessee." But despite the suddenness of the Confederate assault, a number of Federal commanders kept their troops steady. Brigadier General Benjamin M. Prentiss rallied 5,000 Union soldiers along a sunken road and rail fence, using it as a natural breastwork. A series of furious Confederate attacks on the position wasted valuable time and hundreds of lives. Whole ranks fell in a storm of bullets and artillery fire that survivors likened to a swarm of angry hornets. Union resistance finally crumbled under a devastating bombardment by 62 guns, but the stand in the Hornet's Nest gave Grant time to regroup and await the arrival of reinforcements.

MAJOR GENERAL PATRICK RONAYNE CLEBURNE, C.S.A.,
1864. Patrick Cleburne's brigade was in the vanguard of the
Confederate onslaught at Shiloh and lost heavily in the two-
day battle; one of his regiments, the 6th Mississippi, suffered
a casualty rate of 73 percent. Cleburne was born in Ireland and
served as a corporal in the British army before emigrating to
the United States in 1849. Renowned for the risks he took to
inspire his troops, Cleburne died leading a division at Franklin,
Tennessee, on November 30, 1864.

*W*as it not a hard-fought but magnificent and glorious battle? Were
there ever such soldiers as fought that day? No country but ours ever
produced such. It was a battle gallantly won and as stupidly lost.

General Patrick L. Cleburne, C.S.A.
Shiloh

UNION BATTLE LINE, near the Peach Orchard, Shiloh. On the battle's first day, fighting ebbed and flowed through the cotton fields and peach orchard of Manse George, whose cabin is visible at left. When Confederate Colonel Winfield Scott Statham's brigade hesitated to attack, General Johnston rode along the ranks, tapping the men's fixed bayonets with a tin cup, saying, "They are stubborn; we must use the bayonet." Statham's ranks surged forward and broke the Federal line, but Johnston received a mortal wound, and command of the worn-out Confederate forces fell to Beauregard. The next day, Buell's army arrived, Grant ordered an assault, and Beauregard withdrew. Grant lost over 13,000 men at Shiloh, but his determined counterattack moved Union armies a step closer to control of the western theater.

FORT JACKSON, Louisiana. Early in 1862, the Union began a campaign to split the Confederacy in half at the Mississippi River, part of a larger strategy to encircle and strangle the South. Perhaps most important was the capture of New Orleans, the South's largest city and port. In April 1862, combined army and navy forces attacked Forts Jackson and St. Philip, which defended the Mississippi 75 miles below the city. The massive, heavily armed masonry forts, manned by 1400 soldiers under the command of Brigadier General Johnson K. Duncan, were considered all but impregnable. A raft of logs and hulks chained together blocked the river next to the forts, and ironclad Confederate gunboats stood ready to challenge any vessels that managed to make it through.

FORT ST. PHILIP AND FORT JACKSON, Louisiana. A fleet of Union mortar boats pummeled the forts with a five-day bombardment, during which two gunboats forced a narrow way through the hulks. Shortly before dawn on April 24, Captain David G. Farragut's 24 wooden warships, their sides protected by heavy iron chains, successfully ran the gauntlet of the Confederate forts. Avoiding blazing rafts set loose by the Confederate defenders, the Union ships went on to destroy the Rebel gunboats. Farragut arrived off New Orleans on April 25; six days later, Major General Benjamin F. Butler and his troops occupied the city.

DREWRY'S BLUFF, Richmond National Battlefield Park, Virginia. In the spring of 1862, the Confederate capital faced a dual threat. McClellan had finally put his Army of the Potomac on the move, landing 105,000 men on the peninsula between the York and James rivers. As his Federal army edged closer to Richmond, five Union warships sailed up the James. Front-line defense against the flotilla would come at Drewry's Bluff, a mere seven miles downstream from Richmond. A force commanded by Brigadier General G. W. C. Lee, eldest son of Robert E. Lee, expanded Fort Darling, the small earthwork atop the bluff, brought in heavy artillery, and blocked the river channel with sunken boats.

JAMES RIVER AT DREWRY'S BLUFF, Virginia. On May 15, 1862, the Union vessels, led by the ironclads *Monitor* and *Galena*, attempted to blast their way past the Confederate fortifications. The attack failed; the narrow, shallow river hindered maneuvering, and the ironclads' heavy guns could not be sufficiently elevated to hit the Rebel fort 90 feet above the water. The Confederates, on the other hand, were able to depress their guns, scoring 18 hits on the *Galena* alone. The chastened Yankees withdrew after four hours of combat.

GENERAL THOMAS JONATHAN JACKSON, C.S.A. In May 1862, Thomas J. Jackson and Robert E. Lee were generals under Joseph E. Johnston, commander of Confederate forces in the east. Jackson guarded the Shenandoah Valley; Lee directed the defenses of Richmond. As McClellan approached the city, Lee asked Jackson to create a diversion in the Valley. Stonewall responded brilliantly, winning five victories in 30 days over three much larger Federal armies. Stern, religious, and eccentric, Jackson came to be regarded with almost mystical devotion by his hard-marching infantrymen, who called themselves "Jackson's foot cavalry."

F orgetting Jackson's presence, [I] ripped out: "What the h——— are you dodging for? If there is any more of it, you will be halted under this fire for an hour." The sharp tones of a familiar voice produced the desired effect, and the men looked as if they had swallowed ramrods; but I shall never forget the look of reproachful surprise expressed in Jackson's face. He placed his hand on my shoulder, said in a gentle voice, "I am afraid you are a wicked fellow," turned, and rode back to the pike.

General Richard Taylor, C.S.A.
on General Thomas J. "Stonewall" Jackson, C.S.A.

MASSANUTTEN MOUNTAIN, Shenandoah Valley, Virginia. Jackson skillfully used terrain features like 55-mile-long Massanutten Mountain to mask his rapid troop movements. Fearing an advance on Washington, the Union government acted as Lee had hoped, shifting thousands of troops from the Richmond Campaign to the Valley. The former artillery and natural philosophy professor at Virginia Military Institute ended the Valley Campaign with his reputation soaring among generals on both sides. "Jackson was beyond question the greatest soldier developed in our Civil War," Union General Nelson A. Miles declared. "We never knew whether he would descend upon us on the right flank, or the left, or out of the clouds. He was the very embodiment of the genius of war."

KENNON'S MARSH, James River, Virginia

You marched to attack the enemy in his intrenchments with well-directed movements and death-defying valor. You charged upon him in his strong positions, drove him from field to field over a distance of more than 35 miles, and, despite his reinforcements compelled him to seek safety under cover of his gunboats, where he now lies cowering before the army he so lately derided and threatened with entire subjugation.

*President Jefferson Davis
to the Army of Northern Virginia
Seven Days' Campaign*

TREDEGAR IRON WORKS, Richmond, Virginia, 1865. If McClellan had occupied Richmond, the Confederacy's leaders could have moved the government to another city. But the Tredegar Iron Works were irreplaceable. When the war broke out, Tredegar was the only Southern foundry capable of mass-producing artillery tubes and carriages, and its importance soon increased. As the Union blockade tightened and foreign manufacturers hesitated to sell heavy ordnance to the Confederacy, the Yankees gained a potent edge in military hardware. During the war, Northern ironworks manufactured cannon at four times the rate of Southern factories.

TREDEGAR IRON WORKS AND RICHMOND SKYLINE, Virginia. West Point-trained Joseph R. Anderson had been associated with the Tredegar works for nearly 20 years when the Civil War began. Commissioned as a brigadier general in the Confederate army, he returned to supervise the works after being wounded at White Oak Swamp in June 1862. Under his direction, Tredegar tripled its work force and began to supply iron plating for warships, rails for train lines, and 50 percent of all cannon issued to Southern armies. The complex also included a shoe factory, brick factory, sawmill, and tannery.

GENERAL ROBERT EDWARD LEE, C.S.A. On May 31, 1862, General Joseph E. Johnston was hit by a bullet and a shell fragment in the Battle of Fair Oaks, six miles from Richmond. To replace him, Confederate President Jefferson Davis picked Robert E. Lee. Lee was perhaps the most highly regarded officer of the "old army" to join the Confederacy, but his service early in the war had been undistinguished. Upon assuming command, Lee further fortified Richmond, ordered Jackson to join him, and took his newly christened Army of Northern Virginia on the offensive against McClellan.

A *high opinion has been expressed of the strategy of Lee…and it deserves all praise; but the tactics on the field were vastly inferior to the strategy. Indeed, it may be confidently asserted that from Cold Harbor to Malvern Hill…there was nothing but a series of blunders, one after another, all huge. The Confederate commanders knew no more about the topography of the country than they did about Central Africa.*

General Richard Taylor, C.S.A.
on General Robert E. Lee, C.S.A.
Seven Days' Campaign

GAINES'S MILL, Powhite Creek, Virginia. Lee advanced in a week of attacks known as the Seven Days' Campaign. He hoped to isolate and destroy the forces McClellan had deployed north of the Chickahominy River, but his subordinates failed him on June 26 at Mechanicsville and June 27 at Gaines's Mill. Hampered by fatigue, muddy roads, and Union Major General Fitz John Porter's tenacious defensive tactics, Stonewall Jackson and other officers could not put the Yankees to rout. At Gaines's Mill, 6,800 Union and 8,800 Confederate soldiers fell in a bloody, inconclusive struggle. But Lee's boldness had its effect on the Union commander; vastly overestimating Confederate numbers, McClellan abandoned his siege operations and began a retreat to the James River.

MALVERN HILL, Richmond National Battlefield Park, Virginia. Porter's 5th Corps retreated south of the Chickahominy, with Lee and Jackson in pursuit. On July 1, McClellan decided to make one more stand before reaching the cover of his gunboats on the James River, deploying his forces atop a mile-wide plateau called Malvern Hill. Some 100 cannon were positioned almost wheel-to-wheel, many in the vicinity of the West House (right), the headquarters of division commander Brigadier General Darius N. Couch. The Union artillery wreaked havoc on Confederate batteries; when Lee's troops attacked shortly after 5 P.M., salvoes of case shot savaged the Rebel ranks.

MALVERN HILL, Virginia. The Federal line at Malvern Hill was anchored on the left by Porter's men near the Crew House, visible at center on the now-wooded western face of the plateau. As Brigadier General Ambrose R. Wright's Georgia brigade attempted to flank the position, moving across the swampy field in the foreground, the Yankees caught them in a crossfire. Long-range shells from Federal gunboats on the James added to the destruction, and a countercharge by the 14th New York sent the Georgians reeling. The Rebels were thrown back all along the line. "It was not war," Confederate Major General D. H. Hill lamented, "it was murder."

The stupid fact is, that not content with letting me, or others push after the panic stricken enemy, fighting him a big battle, and ending the war...this ass McClellan (so powerful with figures, but weak with men), has brought us all back. It is so like our good old nursery story "the King of France with twice ten thousand men marched up the hill, then marched back down again."

General Philip Kearny, U.S.A.
on General George B. McClellan, U.S.A.
Seven Days' Campaign

MAJOR GENERAL GEORGE BRINTON McCLELLAN, U.S.A. McClellan's change of base from the York to the James, which he called "one of the grandest operations of Military History," was indeed a skillfully conducted fighting retreat. It was also unnecessary. In late May, McClellan had stood six miles from the capital of the Confederacy, with superior numbers, strong supply lines, and confident, well-prepared soldiers who trusted him as they were to trust no other Union general. He relinquished this superb position not because of battle losses, but because he persistently deluded himself that the opposing force outnumbered his and couldn't bring himself to risk decisive action.

HARRISON'S LANDING, Virginia. After repulsing Lee at Malvern Hill, McClellan withdrew his battered Army of the Potomac to Harrison's Landing, his new base on the James, where he badgered President Lincoln and General in Chief Henry Halleck for not less than 100,000 reinforcements. Instead, a thoroughly disenchanted administration began to devise a new strategy, sending Major General John Pope's newly formed Union Army of Virginia south from Washington.

CEDAR MOUNTAIN, Virginia. Knowing that Halleck would soon bolster Pope's 50,000-man army with McClellan's troops, Lee decided to attack Pope while their armies were equally matched. He dispatched Stonewall Jackson to meet the offensive at Cedar Mountain near Culpeper. But Jackson's initial attack on August 9 foundered after Brigadier General Charles S. Winder fell. Union Major General Nathaniel P. Banks sent his 8,000 men in a furious counterattack on Jackson's poorly deployed left and broke through, despite the Confederates' nearly two-to-one advantage. Jackson rode headlong into the woods and rallied his men, and the timely arrival of A. P. Hill's division enabled the Confederates to drive the Federals from the field.

BATTERY HEIGHTS, Manassas National Battlefield Park, Virginia. After Cedar Mountain, Lee pushed northward, dividing his forces to confound slow-moving Federal troops. First Jackson, then Major General James A. Longstreet led their corps in an arc to the west of the Bull Run Mountains. Jackson easily flanked Pope to destroy the Union supply base at Manassas and then took up a formidable position on the old Bull Run battlefield. On the evening of August 28, 1862, he lashed out at Union troops under Brigadier General John Gibbon on the Warrenton Pike. Captain Joseph Campbell's Battery B, 4th United States Artillery, was at the rear of the column when the Rebels struck. As Gibbon formed a line of battle, Campbell unlimbered his six Napoleon guns on a nearby ridge and supported the infantry with salvoes one Confederate likened to "blasts of a hurricane."

MAJOR GENERAL JOHN POPE, U.S.A. Ambitious and vain, Pope led a Missouri campaign in March 1862 that won the upper half of the Mississippi River for the Union and a promotion and transfer to the eastern theater for himself. He had less luck at Manassas. He tried repeatedly on August 29 to smash through Jackson's strong line along an unfinished railroad, but succeeded only in sacrificing thousands of his own soldiers. Even as Longstreet's 30,000 men began to arrive in the area, Pope remained convinced that he faced only half of Lee's army.

A skillful man could have concentrated against me or Jackson, and given us severe battles in detail.... General Pope, sanguine by nature, was not careful enough to keep himself informed about the movements of the enemy.

General James Longstreet, C.S.A.
on General John Pope, U.S.A.
Second Manassas

14TH BROOKLYN MONUMENT, Manassas. At sunset on August 29, a brigade of Union troops trying to flank Jackson ran into Brigadier General John B. Hood's division. The 14th Brooklyn, in the bright red trousers of French *chasseurs*, lost 80 men to an enfilading fire that "wilted the regiment like some invisible breath of plague." The next day, Hood swept across the same ground, forcing Lieutenant Charles Hazlett's battery to abandon its position and virtually annihilating the 5th and 10th New York on Hazlett's left.

53

GENERAL JAMES LONGSTREET, C.S.A. A stalwart but occasionally sluggish commander, James Longstreet served so long with the Army of Northern Virginia that he earned the appellation "Lee's Old War Horse." Many have faulted Longstreet for not attacking with his wing of Lee's army when he arrived at Manassas on August 29. All that day, Jackson's outnumbered command bore the brunt of Pope's offensive.

*T*he heavy fumes of gunpowder hanging about our ranks, as stimulating as sparkling wine, charged the atmosphere with the light and splendor of battle.... As orders were given, the staff, their limbs already closed to their horses' flanks, pressed their spurs, but the electric current overleaped their speedy strides, and twenty-five thousand braves moved in line as by a single impulse.

General James Longstreet, C.S.A.
Second Manassas

CHINN RIDGE, Manassas. Pope ordered another advance on Jackson's lines on the morning of August 30. Jackson again held, and Longstreet finally took the initiative late that afternoon with an assault that overwhelmed the weakened Union left wing. From his headquarters on Buck Hill above the Stone House (center), Pope frantically shifted troops to confront the onslaught. Federal brigades on Chinn Ridge (foreground) were hit in front and flank and gave way in confusion. Union casualties at Second Manassas totaled 16,000, almost twice Confederate losses. As Pope retreated to Washington, Lee prepared to take the war to the North.

NEW YORK MONUMENT, Antietam National Battlefield, Maryland

I looked over my right shoulder and saw the gallant old fellow advancing on the right of our line, almost alone, afoot with his bare sword in his hand, and his face was as black as a thunder cloud; and well it might be, for some of our men, turning their heads toward him, cried out, ''Behind the haystack!'' and he roared out, ''God damn the field officers!'' I shall never cease to admire that magnificent fighting general who advanced with his front line, with his sword bare and ready for use, and his swarthy face, burning eye, and square jaw, though long since lifeless dust, are dear to me.

Lieutenant Thomas L. Livermore, U.S.A.
on General Israel B. Richardson, U.S.A.
Antietam

COLONEL DIXON S. MILES, U.S.A., at headquarters, Harpers Ferry, West Virginia. After crossing the Potomac into Maryland on September 4, 1862, Lee first decided to capture Harpers Ferry and neutralize its 14,000-man garrison. The town was under the command of Colonel Dixon S. Miles, a hard-drinking veteran with 40 years' army service. Miles bungled the defense, causing the largest Union surrender of the war and costing him his reputation and his life.

HARPERS FERRY, West Virginia. Bluffs and mountains enfold Harpers Ferry, built on a peninsula formed by the junction of the Potomac and Shenandoah rivers. Seizing these heights, Stonewall Jackson's forces poured shells on the Federal garrison. On the night of September 14, Colonel Benjamin F. "Grimes" Davis of the 8th New York Cavalry led 1,400 troopers across a pontoon bridge and escaped into Maryland. Colonel Miles was fatally wounded the next day by one of the last shots fired, and 12,500 soldiers and 73 pieces of artillery were surrendered to Jackson.

TURNER'S GAP, South Mountain, Maryland. After Pope's debacle at Manassas, President
Lincoln called upon General McClellan to restore order and morale to the beaten Union army.
A copy of Lee's marching order fell into McClellan's hands, giving him an opportunity to crush
the Confederate forces piece by piece. But on September 14, a few brigades under D. H. Hill
stalled 30,000 Federal troops all morning on South Mountain. Hill got reinforcements in the
afternoon, and it was nightfall before McClellan's army broke through. By then, Jackson had
captured Harpers Ferry, and Lee had begun to gather his scattered forces.

FEDERAL BATTLE LINE, North Woods, Antietam. The Battle of Antietam began at dawn on September 17, 1862, as Major General Joseph Hooker's 1st Corps attacked Lee's left wing near Sharpsburg, Maryland. Hooker held two Pennsylvania brigades commanded by George G. Meade in reserve behind a now-vanished woodlot which stood to the right of the road (center). An hour after the battle began, Meade's men moved south through the woods and, as Confederate artillery shells exploded over and among them, pressed on across a plowed field and a pasture. Six hundred yards from their starting point, the Pennsylvanians entered a cornfield, where 400 of them were struck down amid trampled, bullet-riddled stalks. The field changed hands a dozen times that day.

*S*umner had marched his second division into an ambush. There were some ten Confederate brigades on his front and flank and working rapidly round the rear of his three brigades.... In less time than it takes to tell it, the ground was strewn with the bodies of the dead and wounded.... Nearly two thousand men were disabled in a moment.

Colonel Francis W. Palfrey, U.S.A.
on General Edwin V. Sumner, U.S.A.
Antietam

PHILADELPHIA BRIGADE MONUMENT, West Woods, Antietam. His initial attack blunted, McClellan aimed a second blow at the stubborn Confederate left. Major General Edwin V. Sumner, at age 65 the oldest corps commander in the Union army, led a division of his 2nd Corps into the West Woods. Deployed in three columns only 30 yards apart, the three brigades had no room to maneuver or return fire. Lee had shifted men from his center and right to meet the new threat, and Rebels under Generals Jubal A. Early and Lafayette McLaws shattered the Yankee formation with fire from front, left, and rear. The Philadelphia Brigade was first to break, losing 545 men in 10 minutes.

HAGERSTOWN PIKE AND DUNKER CHURCH, Antietam. The little whitewashed brick church of the Dunkers, a pacifist sect, was at the center of the fighting that crossed and recrossed the Hagerstown Pike. When four regiments of South Carolinians under Brigadier General Joseph B. Kershaw charged troops of Brigadier General George Greene's division, deployed in the field in the foreground, Greene's men cut down the Rebels at point-blank range "like grass before the mower." A second Confederate attack was also repulsed, and at 9:30 A.M., the Union division stormed forward with fixed bayonets and drove the Southerners 300 yards beyond the church.

BLOODY LANE, Antietam. Two Federal divisions spent four hours attacking the center of the Confederate line, where Alabamians and Carolinians held a sunken farm road. Formation after formation crested the rise in front of the road only to be devoured by Confederate volleys. At noon, the line was finally broken, and the 61st New York swung around to fire down the crowded trench, turning it into a "bloody lane." Realizing their men were close to breaking, Confederate generals did whatever they could to stave off defeat. D. H. Hill grabbed a musket and fought in the ranks, and James Longstreet helped man an artillery battery.

EAST EDGE OF THE CORNFIELD, Antietam. Despite the breakthrough at Bloody Lane, McClellan abandoned his efforts to break Lee's left and center. Exhausted troops facing the cornfield remained inactive as the fighting shifted southward to Lee's right flank. Shaken by the unprecedented carnage, McClellan heeded senior officers who discouraged a renewed attack, and continued to hold over 20,000 men of the 5th and 6th Corps in reserve. The cornfield lay between the lines, a gruesome no man's land. "I have heard of the 'dead lying in heaps,'" Emory Upton wrote his sister, "but never saw it till at this battle."

BURNSIDE'S BRIDGE, Antietam. McClellan aimed his third offensive at a stone bridge spanning Antietam Creek opposite Lee's right flank. But all morning, a mere 500 Confederate soldiers commanded by a Georgia politician, Brigadier General Robert A. Toombs, held off 11,000 Federals under Major General Ambrose E. Burnside. Two Union assaults were shot to pieces before reaching the bridge. At 1 P.M., a concerted rush across the span by the 51st New York and 51st Pennsylvania finally forced the Georgian sharpshooters to retreat. Once across, however, Burnside stalled again.

SHERRICK HOUSE AND OTTO HOUSE, Antietam. It was midafternoon before Burnside's 9th Corps resumed its ponderous advance on Sharpsburg and the weakest point in Lee's line. When Brigadier General Orlando B. Willcox's division moved up the road past the homes of John Otto (top) and Joseph Sherrick (bottom), only detachments of skirmishers and artillerists lay between the Yankees and Sharpsburg. But they slowed the bluecoats long enough for A. P. Hill's division, which had marched 17 miles from Harpers Ferry in under eight hours, to strike Burnside's left and bring the entire Union advance to a sudden halt. The bloodiest day of combat in the Civil War ended in a tactical draw, but Lee, his army decimated, retreated south across the Potomac the following night.

GENERAL BRAXTON BRAGG, C.S.A. Braxton Bragg, whose forces invaded Kentucky in August 1862, was an ill-tempered perfectionist and an iron disciplinarian whose ugly personality may have done as much harm to the Confederate cause in the west as his flawed generalship. "He loved to crush the spirit of his men," one private recalled. "Not a single soldier in the whole army ever loved or respected him." Typically, Bragg blamed the failure of his Kentucky campaign on the lack of support from the populace.

*I*n not returning to Perryville and resuming the battle, he lost for the Confederacy perhaps the only opportunity it ever had of fighting a great battle with a decisive preponderance in numbers and the character of its troops.

General Charles C. Gilbert, U.S.A.
on General Braxton Bragg, C.S.A.
Perryville

UNION LEFT FLANK, Perryville Battlefield, Kentucky. Both commanding officers at Perryville were hampered by poor reconnaissance. Bragg thought he had met a small Federal force and brought only a third of his troops into action. Union Major General Don Carlos Buell believed his Army of the Ohio faced Bragg's entire command; in fact, he outnumbered them two to one. On October 8, 1862, the Confederates took the initiative. Major General Benjamin F. Cheatham's division plowed through two Federal brigades but foundered against a second Union line bolstered by artillery on the hill west of the Benton Road (center).

FEDERAL DIVISION AT DRILL, Blue Springs, Tennessee. Following Napoleonic principles, Civil War soldiers performed frequent close-order drills in formations of companies, regiments, brigades, and divisions. The Union division shown here is drawn up in columns of brigades, each brigade in columns of regiments. The division's artillery has unlimbered right of the line, and skirmishers have deployed to the front. In actual battle, the skirmish line would be several hundred yards ahead of the main body; otherwise the formation would appear the same.

CONFEDERATE CEMETERY, Perryville. Atop a knoll where casualties were very heavy, 435 Confederate dead were later interred. Here Brigadier General George E. Maney's brigade spearheaded a charge that smashed through the Federal line commanded by Brigadier General James S. Jackson. Jackson went down with a fatal wound, as did one of his subordinate generals, William R. Terrill. The Virginia-born Terrill had been ostracized by his family when he chose to fight for the North. His brother, a Confederate colonel, died in action in 1864.

SHAKER VILLAGE OF PLEASANT HILL, Kentucky. After a Union counterattack had thrown them back over a mile, Bragg's Confederates retreated in the night. The key border state of Kentucky, birthplace of both Abraham Lincoln and Jefferson Davis, remained in Union control. Pleasant Hill, a prosperous Shaker settlement, lay 16 miles northeast of Perryville. Despite their antislavery views, the Shakers provided food and medical supplies to Yankees and Rebels alike, though they were careful to conceal most of their livestock from the eyes of hungry soldiers. Bragg's failure had a devastating effect on the town's economy, dependent on trade with Southern markets.

BRIGADIER GENERAL RUFUS INGALLS, U.S.A., 1864. Although he never led troops in
battle, Ingalls played a crucial role in the war. As chief quartermaster of the Army of the Potomac,
Ingalls's task was immense: to support one of the world's largest armies as it moved through
conquered territory. But the stocky West Point classmate of Grant never seemed ruffled. One
of General Meade's staff officers thought that Ingalls maneuvered his mile-long wagon trains
over rutted Virginia roads "as if they were perambulators on a smooth sidewalk."

FREDERICKSBURG, Virginia. Disgusted with McClellan's failure to quickly cross the Potomac and march on Lee while fall weather held, Lincoln dismissed him and placed Burnside in command of the Army of the Potomac on November 7, 1862. Burnside rapidly moved his 110,000 men to positions near Fredericksburg, where he hoped to cross the Rappahannock River. While the Federal commander waited for pontoon bridges, Lee secured strong positions on the heights west of the town. When Union troops finally began their crossing on December 11, 1,600 Rebel troops posted in Fredericksburg severely hindered them for 12 hours. A bombardment from 100 Federal cannon set Fredericksburg on fire but failed to dislodge the riflemen. On the afternoon of December 12, several Union regiments were rowed across the river and secured the town.

NATIONAL CEMETERY, Marye's Heights, Fredericksburg, Virginia. On December 13, Burnside could at last begin an assault on Lee's lines. One Confederate soldier called Burnside's attack on Marye's Heights "a butchery," and so it was. Fully exposed to Confederate guns, the Federal troops had to cross a plain two miles wide. Charge after charge ended in carnage. Today a national cemetery on the crest contains the remains of many of the 7,000 Union soldiers who fell. The statue at upper right portrays Brigadier General Andrew A. Humphreys, whose division made one of the day's final assaults. When the hopeless order arrived, Humphreys turned to his staff and said, "Gentlemen, I shall lead the charge. I presume, of course, you will wish to ride with me." Humphreys came back unscathed, but not one Union soldier reached the stone wall on Marye's Heights that day. Burnside retreated across the Rappahannock on December 15.

HAZEN MONUMENT, Stones River National Battlefield, Tennessee. One of the western theater's largest battles began near Murfreesboro, Tennessee, on the last day of 1862, when Braxton Bragg surprised and routed the right flank of Major General William S. Rosecrans's Army of the Cumberland. The Union right folded back on the left, then rallied near the Round Forest. Here Colonel William B. Hazen's brigade helped hold the line until night ended the repeated Confederate assaults. A stone monument from 1863, said to be the nation's oldest Civil War memorial, marks the graves of 55 men lost in Hazen's brigade that day.

NASHVILLE PIKE AND NATIONAL CEMETERY, Stones River. The final Union line on December 31 ran just south of and parallel to the Nashville Pike (center). Following the brutal first day, both Bragg and Rosecrans waited before renewing the battle. On January 2, Major General Thomas L. Crittenden's men repulsed a Confederate attack east of Stones River with great slaughter, and Bragg retreated. Twenty thousand men were killed or wounded at Murfreesboro; the casualty rate of one soldier in three caused Bragg and Rosecrans to spend months rebuilding their armies.

There are Generals as young with less claim for that distinction, and no veteran in age has ever shown more coolness and better judgment in the sphere of his duty.

General J. E. B. Stuart, C.S.A.
on Major John Pelham, C.S.A

MAJOR JOHN PELHAM, C.S.A. Alabamian John Pelham, shown here in his West Point furlough uniform, combined boyish good looks with military skills that made him one of the Confederacy's most noted artillery commanders. His bravery in the Battle of Fredericksburg, where his guns enfiladed the Union line, moved Robert E. Lee to exclaim, "It is glorious to see such courage in one so young." Pelham's death at 25 in the Battle of Kelly's Ford was both heroic and senseless; eager to enter the fray, he galloped forward with charging Virginia cavalrymen and was struck down by an exploding shell.

KELLY'S FORD, Rappahannock River, Virginia. When "Fighting Joe" Hooker replaced Burnside as commander of the Army of the Potomac early in 1863, he determined to group his horse soldiers, previously scattered among infantry divisions, in a unified command. The new Cavalry Corps proved Hooker's good sense on March 17 when they met a detachment of General J. E. B. "Jeb" Stuart's famous troopers at Kelly's Ford. The fight pitted Brigadier General William W. Averell against his old West Point friend, Fitzhugh Lee, Robert E. Lee's nephew. The Yankee troopers surprised the Rebels by fighting to a draw before retreating—a display of tenacity that boded ill for the continued supremacy of Stuart's horsemen.

CHANCELLOR CEMETERY, Chancellorsville Battlefield, Fredericksburg and Spotsylvania National Military Park, Virginia. Over the long winter encampment of 1862-63, Hooker rebuilt the Army of the Potomac, replacing lost troops and restoring morale. When he moved against Lee that spring, he brought 135,000 men against Lee's 60,000. The armies met west of Fredericksburg in the dense woods of the Wilderness. Fairview Heights, a clearing that held the Chancellor family cemetery, was one of the few places offering a view over the battlefield.

CONFLUENCE OF THE RAPIDAN AND RAPPAHANNOCK RIVERS, north of Chancellorsville, Virginia. Hooker's carefully planned spring offensive went well at first. While the Union left wing under Major General John Sedgwick maintained its pressure on Lee at Fredericksburg, three army corps made a sweeping flank march to the northwest, forded the Rappahannock and Rapidan rivers, and emerged in the Wilderness on Lee's left and rear. With the bulk of his forces at Chancellorsville, the over-confident Hooker declared: "The enemy must either ingloriously fly or come out from behind his entrenchments and give us battle on our own ground, where certain destruction awaits him."

In the midst of this awful scene General Lee...rode to the front of his advancing battalions.... The fierce soldiers, with their faces blackened with the smoke of battle, the wounded, crawling with feeble limbs from the fury of the devouring flames, all seemed possessed with a common impulse. One long, unbroken cheer... rose high above the roar of battle and hailed the presence of the victorious chief. He sat in the full realization of all that soldiers dream of—triumph; and as I looked on him in the complete fruition of the success which his genius, courage, and confidence in his army had won, I thought that it must have been from some such scene that men in ancient days ascended to the dignity of the gods.

Colonel Charles Marshall, C.S.A.
on General Robert E. Lee, C.S.A.
Chancellorsville

HAZEL GROVE, Chancellorsville. As the armies closed for battle on May 1, Hooker suddenly turned lethargic. Sensing hesitation, Lee seized the initiative. But the fight was to cost the South dearly. After executing a brilliant flank march that smashed Hooker's right, Stonewall Jackson was mortally wounded at dusk on the second day by Confederate soldiers who mistook the general's party for Federal cavalry. Lee placed Jeb Stuart in acting command of Jackson's corps. On May 3, Stuart saw that the Federals had abandoned Hazel Grove, a strategic ridge, and dispatched Colonel E. Porter Alexander to occupy it with 30 cannon.

CHANCELLOR HOUSE FOUNDATIONS, Chancellorsville. Located at a crucial road junction, the rambling Chancellor House was Hooker's headquarters and the linchpin of his defensive line. On the morning of May 3, Alexander's artillery commenced to pound Federal positions at Fairview Heights and Chancellorsville. Hooker himself was knocked unconscious when a shell fragment splintered a wooden porch post against which he was leaning. When he came to, he gave orders to withdraw toward the Rappahannock. As they retreated through the clearing, many Yankee soldiers who saw their dazed commander thought that he was simply in a drunken stupor.

*G*eneral Hooker has disappointed all his friends by failing to show his fighting qualities at the pinch. He was more cautious and took to digging quicker even than McClellan, thus proving that a man may talk very big when he has no responsibility, but that it is quite a different thing, acting when you are responsible.

General George G. Meade, U.S.A.
on General Joseph Hooker, U.S.A.
Chancellorsville

SALEM CHURCH, Fredericksburg and Spotsylvania National Military Park, Virginia. As Hooker and Lee clashed at Chancellorsville, Sedgwick's 6th Corps brushed aside Brigadier General Jubal Early's 10,000 Rebel troops on Marye's Heights. Only nine miles separated Sedgwick from Chancellorsville, where his arrival might well have won the battle for the North. But at Salem Church, four miles west of Fredericksburg, Brigadier General Cadmus M. Wilcox's Alabama brigade stopped Sedgwick's men. Lee hastily dispatched a division under Lafayette McLaws to join Wilcox, ending Hooker's grandiose pincer movement.

MAJOR GENERAL JOSEPH HOOKER, U.S.A. Hooker's ingenious strategy had raised Union hopes, making his failure to defeat Lee especially disappointing. Some critics alleged that drinking caused the high-living commander's blunders at Chancellorsville. Others, noting that Hooker had publicly forsworn liquor before the campaign, suggested that abstinence jangled his nerves. Perhaps Hooker himself put it best when he said, "For once, I lost confidence in Hooker." Amid the recriminations, Lincoln renewed the search for a general fit to lead the Army of the Potomac.

BEVERLY FORD, Rappahannock River, Brandy Station Battlefield, Virginia. At daylight on June 9, 1863, Brigadier General Alfred Pleasonton launched the Army of the Potomac's Cavalry Corps in a surprise attack on Jeb Stuart's Southern horsemen encamped near Brandy Station. Faulty execution marred the three-pronged assault; nonetheless, when General John Buford's division charged across Beverly Ford, the Confederates were taken unawares. One of the first Federal casualties was Colonel "Grimes" Davis, who had led the breakout at Harpers Ferry.

THE BARBOUR HOUSE, "BEAUREGARD," Brandy Station. The Barbour House had been renamed in 1861 in honor of the victor of First Manassas. From "Beauregard," Robert E. Lee witnessed the later stages of the Battle of Brandy Station, and was in fact in some danger as elements of the 1st New Jersey Cavalry charged near the house. Lee's second son, Brigadier General W. H. F. "Rooney" Lee, was severely wounded leading one of Stuart's brigades in the fight.

MAJOR GENERAL JAMES EWELL BROWN STUART, C.S.A.
With his plumed hat, gold sash, and flowing cape, Jeb Stuart
looked and acted the part of the ideal cavalry commander. In
the first two years of war, Stuart's raids harried Lee's opponents
and gained intelligence at critical moments. But after his
embarrassment at Brandy Station, Stuart rashly tried to regain
lost glory at Gettysburg. On June 25, he abandoned Lee for a
far-ranging raid through Maryland and Pennsylvania that left
the Confederate commander without his "eyes and ears" for
a full week.

*T*his occurred in the hot fight of Fleetwood Hill...when he was almost surrounded by the heavy masses of the enemy's cavalry, and very nearly cut off.... His voice was curt, harsh, imperious, admitting no reply. The veins in his forehead grew black, and the man looked "dangerous." If an officer failed him at such moments, he never forgave him.

Captain John Esten Cooke, C.S.A.
on General J. E. B. Stuart, C.S.A.
Brandy Station

FLEETWOOD HILL, Brandy Station. Charge and countercharge swept over Fleetwood Hill at Brandy Station, the Civil War's largest cavalry battle. In the day-long melee, regimental order often disintegrated into individual combat with saber and revolver. Stuart, at his best in a crisis, blunted an attack by Brigadier General David M. Gregg's division on the southern edge of Fleetwood Hill. The 35th Virginia Battalion overran three Union cannon on the rise in the foreground and sabered the gunners. The Confederates won the day, but Pleasonton had further demonstrated the competence of the Union cavalry.

UNITED STATES NAVY MEMORIAL, Vicksburg National Military Park, Mississippi

*T*he cannonading from the hundreds of guns on land and water was terrific and deafening, and the air was alive with screaming shot and bursting shell.... Suddenly every gun ceased firing along Grant's front, except from the covered sharpshooters, who could overshoot the charging Federals who rose and moved toward the Confederate lines for a space of three and a half miles around. The scene was a grand one, the rough hills and valleys turning blue and appearing alive with the assaulting Federals.

General Stephen D. Lee, C.S.A.
Vicksburg

FORT HILL, Vicksburg. A victory at Vicksburg would sever Texas, Arkansas, and Louisiana from the Confederacy and make the Mississippi a Yankee river. For over a year, the heavily fortified city defied Federal assaults by land and water. In April 1863, Grant began a relentless campaign, bringing 70,000 Union troops against Philadelphia-born Lieutenant General John C. Pemberton's 20,000-man garrison. Fort Hill anchored the left flank of the Southern line; its position high atop the bluffs had been the site of a military outpost as early as 1791, when Spain ruled the river.

SIEGE LINES, Old Graveyard Road, Vicksburg. Grant won five consecutive victories in 20 days as he brought his army from Port Gibson, Mississippi, to Vicksburg. On May 19 and 22, 1863, he attempted to carry the defenses by storm. Both assaults were repulsed; Union losses totaled more than 4,000 to Pemberton's 750. Some of the heaviest combat occurred when soldiers of Sherman's 15th Corps advanced up the Old Graveyard Road to the Stockade Redan, a strong point at the northeast corner of the nine-mile-long line of Confederate earthworks.

UNION BOMBPROOFS, near the Shirley House, Vicksburg. Undeterred by the failed assaults, Grant besieged the city for six weeks. Soldiers of the 45th Illinois honeycombed a hillside near the Shirley House with bombproof shelters to protect themselves during Rebel shelling. Vicksburg fell under a far deadlier bombardment from Union batteries on land and ironclad gunboats on the Mississippi, causing civilians to excavate an estimated 500 "caves" in the hills, many furnished with belongings from their shattered homes.

UNITED STATES NAVY MONUMENT AND RIVER BLUFFS, Vicksburg. On the night of April 16, 1863, Rear Admiral David Porter led his gunboats and a convoy of troops and supplies past Vicksburg's formidable batteries to Grant's base of operations downriver. Once Grant laid siege to the town, Porter's ships periodically engaged the Confederate fortifications. When the Confederates unconditionally surrendered to Grant on July 4, Porter could take much of the credit.

LOCOMOTIVE, UNITED STATES MILITARY RAILROAD. Having gained control of the South's major rivers, Union armies moved against the main rail lines. The American Civil War was the first war in which railroads played a significant role. The transport of troops, ammunition, and supplies by rail not only added a new mobility to strategy, but caused entire campaigns to be guided by the seizure or destruction of rail lines and junctions. Brigadier General Herman Haupt, a civil engineer and superintendent of the Pennsylvania Railroad, masterminded the network of United States Military Railroads.

BIG BLACK RIVER BRIDGE FOUNDATIONS AND MODERN BRIDGE, near Bovina, Mississippi. Battles along the Southern Mississippi Railroad were an important part of the Vicksburg Campaign. In April 1863, Union Colonel Benjamin H. Grierson led a cavalry raid 100 miles into Mississippi to cut the rail line in the middle of the state. Grant's capture of Jackson on May 14 not only secured the state capital, but ended all railroad supplies to Pemberton's army at Vicksburg. After a raging conflict on May 17 at a bend in the Big Black River, Confederate Brigadier General John S. Bowen retreated to Vicksburg, burning the railroad bridges behind him. But Union engineers built pontoons in a matter of hours, and Federal troops soon marched 15 miles to the outskirts of Vicksburg.

LITTLE ROUND TOP, Gettysburg National Military Park, Pennsylvania

*S*uch a scene of carnage I never imagined.... Dead horses, shattered carriages, dead and dying men, in all the last agonies of death for two full hours, would have paralyzed anyone not trained to the ''butcher trade.'' I was fighting for my native state, and before I went in thought of those at home I so dearly love. If Gettysburg was lost all was lost for them.

General Alexander Hays, U.S.A.
Gettysburg

SOUTH FROM MUMMASBURG ROAD, Gettysburg. Emboldened by success at Chancellorsville, Lee invaded Pennsylvania in June. Lincoln answered with yet another change of command in the Army of the Potomac, replacing Hooker with George G. Meade. As the two huge armies edged toward each other, Lee and Meade knew they would meet in a decisive battle. But neither planned Gettysburg as the field or July 1, 1863, as the day. Lee's divided forces were simply to rendezvous there, but when divisions under A. P. Hill arrived on July 1, they chanced upon Brigadier General John Buford's Union cavalry. Buford's men, fighting dismounted, valiantly held lines near the Mummasburg Road until Major General John F. Reynold's 1st Corps arrived. In the afternoon, as the battle escalated, Lee's troops pushed the Federals south through the town to a series of ridges.

PEACH ORCHARD SALIENT, Gettysburg. By evening, the Union army formed a strong line two miles long, curving west and south from Culp's Hill to Cemetery Ridge and the Round Tops. On July 2, Union Major General Daniel E. Sickles, holding the south end, moved his 3rd Corps forward without Meade's approval. Sickles intended his new line, running from the Peach Orchard (right) along the Emmitsburg Road (center), to improve his defensive position. In fact, he jeopardized the entire Federal army. Just after 6 P.M., Brigadier General William Barksdale's Mississippians rushed past the Sherfy barn (lower left) and through the peach trees, breaking Sickles's line and surging toward Cemetery Ridge. Other Rebels headed for the Round Tops (top), hoping to turn the Yankees' left flank.

MAJOR GENERAL GEORGE GORDON MEADE, U.S.A.
A military engineer and veteran of the Mexican War, Meade
was known as a solid if not inspirational division commander.
No one expected Lincoln to choose him for the Union Army's
most important field command. Meade was 47 years old at the
time of Gettysburg, but the strain of command made him
appear far older.

From the time I took command till to-day, now over ten days, I have not changed my clothes, have not had a regular night's rest, and many nights not a wink of sleep, and for several days did not even wash my face and hands, no regular food, and all the time in a great state of mental anxiety. Indeed, I think I have lived as much in this time as in the last thirty years.

General George G. Meade, U.S.A.
Gettysburg

LITTLE ROUND TOP AND VALLEY OF DEATH, Gettysburg. The very size of the Gettysburg battle-field made it difficult for Meade and Lee to exert tactical control over their subordinates. Officers' snap decisions frequently determined the course of battle. When Meade's topographical engineer, Brigadier General Gouverneur Kemble Warren, found the crest of Little Round Top undefended against Longstreet's advance, he took the initiative, ordering troops from the 5th Corps to secure the threaten-ed hill. In the subsequent fight on the boulder-strewn slopes, two brigades of the 5th Corps prevented the Confederates from flanking the Federal left and saved the Union from defeat.

EAST FROM SEMINARY RIDGE TO CEMETERY RIDGE, Gettysburg. On July 3, Lee commanded Longstreet to attack the Union center along Cemetery Ridge with divisions led by Generals George Pickett, Isaac Trimble, and Johnston Pettigrew. This decision struck many officers as badly flawed. Porter Alexander, whose guns prepared the way for the advance with a tremendous barrage of the Union line, thought "the point selected for Pickett's attack was very badly chosen—almost as badly chosen as it was possible to be."

WEST FROM THE ANGLE TO SEMINARY RIDGE, Gettysburg. Longstreet's assault on the Union center has gone down in history as Pickett's Charge, the "high-water mark" of the Confederacy. Several hundred Confederates led by Brigadier General Lewis A. Armistead pierced the Union line between the Copse of Trees and The Angle (center), but were thrown back almost at once. The grit and gallantry with which the Federal 2nd Corps met and repulsed the habitually victorious troops of the Army of Northern Virginia signaled a turning point in the morale of both armies. Longstreet's retreating troops washed up around Lee. Shaken and apologetic, the Rebel commander began his withdrawal the next day, July 4.

VINIARD FIELD, Chickamauga, Chickamauga and Chattanooga National Military Park, Georgia. Strengthened by Longstreet's corps, which Jefferson Davis shifted west after Gettysburg, Braxton Bragg sought to trap William Rosecrans's Army of the Cumberland in the Georgia hills south of Chattanooga, Tennessee. Battle was joined on September 19, 1863, near Chickamauga Creek, and although casualties quickly mounted, neither side gained an advantage. Viniard Field saw desperate fighting late in the day, as a Confederate division led by John Hood crashed through Brigadier General William P. Carlin's brigade. In the heat of the clash, the 2nd Minnesota Battery cut the fuses of their shells so short that they exploded among the Union ranks.

GEORGIA MONUMENT, Chickamauga. Longstreet broke the standoff at Chickamauga at noon on September 20, driving 23,000 Confederates through a quarter-mile gap in Rosecrans's line and crushing the Union right. Brigadier General Henry L. Benning's Georgia brigade played a conspicuous role in the attack. Benning, a former associate justice of the Georgia Supreme Court, had three horses killed under him in the charge. His last mount of the day was an artillery horse, still in harness, that had been cut from the traces of a captured Union limber.

MAJOR GENERAL ALEXANDER MCDOWELL MCCOOK, U.S.A. Alexander McCook belonged to an Ohio clan dubbed the "Fighting McCooks"; his father and four brothers died serving the Union. A genial man, fond of singing and entertaining, McCook looked the part of a general. He had taught infantry tactics at West Point before the war, but he proved a poor field commander. Not long before Chickamauga, Union General John Beatty described him as a "blockhead" and commented, "It is astonishing to me that he should be permitted to retain command of a corps for a single hour." McCook, swept away in the rout of his 20th Corps at Chickamauga, was never given another field command.

BROTHERTON FIELD, Chickamauga. Tom Brotherton, a Confederate private whose family owned a 700-acre tract at Chickamauga, gave Longstreet the lay of the land before his attack. The fields north of the Brotherton Cabin were already covered with dead from the first day's fighting, when the guns of Captain Alanson Stevens's Independent Battery, Pennsylvania Artillery (center) had helped slow the charge of Confederate Major General Alexander P. Stewart's division. Longstreet's advance across the field on September 20 was easier; a mix-up in orders had left the gap in the Union line that allowed his decisive assault.

WILDER MONUMENT, Chickamauga. Colonel John T. Wilder's brigade of mounted infantry defended the Union right on both days of the battle. Wilder's troops carried new Spencer rifles, lever-action repeaters that could fire seven shots without reloading. Most of the Federal army gave way before Longstreet's onslaught "like flecks of foam upon a river," but with the Spencers' firepower Wilder and his men held their ground. "The effect was awful," Wilder later wrote. "The head of the attacking column seemed to melt away or sink into the earth."

*A*ll this talk about generalship displayed on either side was sheer nonsense. There was no generalship in it. It was a soldier's fight purely, wherein the only question involved was the question of endurance. The two armies came together like two wild beasts, and each fought as long as it could stand up in a knock-down-and-drag-out encounter. If there had been any high order of generalship displayed the disasters to both armies might have been less.

Colonel John T. Wilder, U.S.A.
Chickamauga

KELLY HOUSE AND FIELD, Chickamauga. Brigadier General Absalom Baird's division manned a salient at the Kelly House, covering Rosecrans's retreat to Chattanooga, 10 miles north between Missionary Ridge (center) and Lookout Mountain (top). Baird reported that his men were "fired into from every point of the compass.... Still we held our position, yielding not an inch." Abraham Lincoln's brother-in-law, Brigadier General Benjamin Hardin Helm, was fatally wounded leading a Confederate brigade against the salient. At the outbreak of hostilities, the Kentucky lawyer had declined the President's offer of a commission in the Union army.

LOOKOUT MOUNTAIN, Tennessee. In October 1863, Grant took control of the Federal forces in Chattanooga, the crucial rail junction on the Tennessee River besieged since Chickamauga. Grant's operations in November challenged Bragg's lines south and east of the city. With two corps swiftly transported by rail from Virginia, Joseph Hooker was given the task of clearing the Confederates from the precipitous crest of Lookout Mountain, high above the city. Photographer George N. Barnard, who later documented Sherman's Atlanta Campaign, took this image of Lookout Point, the mountain's northern tip.

NEW YORK MONUMENT, Point Park, Lookout Mountain. Hooker's three divisions closed in on their objective on the morning of November 24, 1863, taking advantage of low-lying clouds that concealed their movements from the Confederates. Bragg had shifted troops from the mountain to bolster his main line on Missionary Ridge, four miles to the east, giving Hooker a decisive advantage in numbers. The "Battle Above the Clouds" raged throughout the day on a small plateau beneath the mountain's sheer northern face.

CRAVENS HOUSE, Lookout Mountain. For two hours, Confederate General Edward C. Walthall's brigade battled Hooker's troops from behind entrenchments near the shell-torn Cravens farmhouse, then fell back 400 yards to a second line of trenches. Rebel reinforcements rushed to the scene and held the second line until night. The next morning, the Federals found their enemy had retreated under cover of darkness. The 8th Kentucky hoisted their flag over Lookout Mountain, Hooker reported, "amid the wild and prolonged cheers of the men whose dauntless valor had borne it to that point."

OHIO STATE MONUMENT, Missionary Ridge. On November 25, Grant commenced a seemingly impossible assault on heavily defended Missionary Ridge, where the Rebels had spent two months preparing positions. But as 23,000 soldiers under Major General George H. Thomas advanced, they discovered that Bragg's engineers had laid out the strongest line of entrenchments on the summit rather than the military crest of the ridge. This gave the Union troops a clear approach out of the line of fire. Once started, there was no stopping the enthusiastic Yankees. Led by Brigadier General Thomas J. Wood and Major General Philip H. Sheridan, they kept moving until the Confederate position was taken. Bragg's defeat relinquished a strategic nerve center and gave Sherman the springboard for his march to Atlanta.

WELFORD HOUSE, UNION 6TH CORPS HEADQUARTERS, winter 1863-64, near Brandy
Station, Virginia

In the "wilderness" there was no room for grand strategy, or even minor tactics; but the fighting was desperate.... On the night of May 7th both parties paused, appalled by the fearful slaughter; but General Grant commanded "Forward by the left flank." That was, in my judgment, the supreme moment of his life: undismayed, with a full comprehension of the importance of the work in which he was engaged, feeling as keen a sympathy for the dead and wounded as any one, and without stopping to count his numbers, he gave his orders calmly, specifically, and absolutely—"Forward to Spotsylvania."

General William T. Sherman, U.S.A.
on General Ulysses S. Grant, U.S.A.
Wilderness Campaign

BRIGADIER GENERAL THOMAS LAFAYETTE ROSSER,
C.S.A. The spring of 1864 found Tom Rosser's "Laurel Brigade"
probing the flanks of the Union army as Grant marched
into central Virginia. In the grueling weeks of the Wilderness
Campaign, Rosser discovered that seasoned Northern troopers
no longer flinched at his hell-for-leather tactics.

My bright dream that Rosser was one of the first calvery Generals in our service is gone. He is no General at all. As brave a man as ever drew breath, but knows no more about putting a command into a fight than a school boy. We have lost confidence in him so fast that he can't get a good fight out of us any more unless we know positively what we are fighting.

Captain Frank Myers, C.S.A.
on General Thomas L. Rosser, C.S.A.
Wilderness Campaign

SAUNDERS FIELD, Wilderness Battlefield, Fredericksburg and Spotsylvania National Military Park, Virginia. A month of nearly continuous fighting began on May 5, 1864, as Grant and Lee collided in a two-day battle in the thickets of the Wilderness. Some of the heaviest combat took place in Saunders Field when four Union regiments in exotic Zouave uniforms charged across the clearing against entrenched Confederates of Lieutenant General Richard S. Ewell's corps. The "Zouave Brigade" was repelled, and many wounded perished when the woods and field caught fire.

BREVET MAJOR GENERAL EMORY UPTON, U.S.A.
A vicious, week-long battle, the second major engagement of
the Wilderness Campaign, came at the Spotsylvania Court
House crossroads. On May 10, Emory Upton's tactically brilliant
charge on the "Mule Shoe" salient was repulsed because it lacked
support. But Upton's temporary success encouraged Grant to
try a much larger assault two days later and won the young West
Pointer a long-deserved brigadier's star.

*N*o duty was omitted. Drill, discipline, and order were exacted from all, and supervised by him in all the regiments under his command. Tactics and formations for battle were most carefully studied, and nothing was left to chance.... It soon came to be understood that Upton's brigade must lead all attacks and assaults made within his reach, and, what was of still greater credit to him, he rarely failed to carry the enemy's position.

General James T. Wilson, U.S.A.
on General Emory Upton, U.S.A.
Wilderness Campaign

SITE OF THE ADAMS HOUSE, Cold Harbor Battlefield, Virginia. After being repelled at Spotsylvania, Grant attempted to break through Lee's entrenchments at Cold Harbor. Fought on a portion of the old Gaines's Mill battlefield, the three-day Union attack wasted the lives of seasoned officers and men. The only success came on June 3, when Brigadier General Francis C. Barlow's division of the 2nd Corps, attacking across the fields beyond the Adams House (upper center), briefly overran a portion of the Confederate works. Troops from Maryland and Florida soon drove the Yankees out and restored the line.

NATIONAL CEMETERY AND GARTHRIGHT HOUSE, Cold Harbor, Richmond National Battlefield Park, Virginia. The Garthright House (at edge of woods) stood just behind the lines of the Union 6th Corps at Cold Harbor and served as a field hospital for some of the Union's 7,000 casualties. Even Grant was shaken by the morale-crippling losses, calling Cold Harbor "the only battle I ever fought that I would not fight over again under the circumstances."

MAJOR GENERAL WINFIELD SCOTT HANCOCK, U.S.A., with staff near Cold Harbor, June 10, 1864. "Hancock the Superb" (center), as McClellan had called him, commanded the 2nd Corps, widely regarded as the best in Grant's army. Hancock's men broke Pickett's charge at Gettysburg, and until 1864, they never lost a gun or a flag. But the month-long campaign from the Rapidan to the James shattered the corps, which bore 16,000 of the 50,000 casualties in Grant's army. Hancock himself endured the constant pain of an unhealed wound from Gettysburg.

CITY POINT, near Hopewell, Virginia. After the battles in the Wilderness, Grant wheeled his army to the south and west to attack the crucial rail hub of Petersburg, Virginia. Lee's troops dug in around the town, and a 10-month siege began. Grant transformed City Point, a sleepy town at the confluence of the Appomattox and James rivers, into a mammoth supply base. The United States Military Railroad hauled thousands of tons of supplies from City Point's wharves to the Union trenches ringing Petersburg.

APPOMATTOX MANOR AND GRANT'S HEADQUARTERS, City Point. While many senior officers, including Chief Quartermaster Rufus Ingalls, lived at "Appomattox Manor," a sprawling plantation house, Grant chose humbler quarters: a tent until November, then a cabin (right) erected on the estate. There he planned the grand offensive on all fronts to end the war by spring.

FORT STEDMAN, Petersburg National Battlefield, Virginia

One of the most anxious periods of my experience during the rebellion was the last few weeks before Petersburg. I felt that the situation of the Confederate army was such that they would try to make an escape at the earliest practicable moment, and I was afraid, every morning, that I would awake from my sleep to hear that Lee had gone, and that nothing was left but a picket line.... I knew he could move much more lightly and more rapidly than I, and that, if he got a start, he would leave me behind so that we would have the same army to fight again farther south—and the war might be prolonged another year.

General Ulysses S. Grant, U.S.A.
Petersburg

MAJOR GENERAL WILLIAM TECUMSEH SHERMAN, U.S.A., with corps commanders. With his own forces stalled at Petersburg, Grant called on the western armies to sever Lee's last supply routes. "Cump" Sherman (seated, second from left), Grant's former protégé, began with an ingenious feinting and flanking campaign from Chattanooga to Atlanta during the summer of 1864. On his marches through Georgia and South Carolina, Sherman cut loose from supply bases and let his armies live off the land. This age-old strategy put him in the vanguard of "modern" military leadership.

KENNESAW MOUNTAIN, Kennesaw Mountain National Battlefield Park, Georgia. Confederate General Joseph E. Johnston contested the southward advance of Sherman's three armies in a series of bloody engagements, thwarting Federal efforts to turn his left, but always retreating closer to Atlanta. On June 27, 1864, Sherman struck Johnston, sending three corps against a strong Confederate position on Kennesaw Mountain, 20 miles northwest of Atlanta. The attack was a western version of Cold Harbor. "It became," one Union soldier wrote, "a slaughter of men like beasts in the shambles." But neither Johnston nor his replacement John Hood could stop Sherman, whose armies entered Atlanta on September 2.

MONOCACY BATTLEFIELD, near Frederick, Maryland. In July 1864, Lee sent Lieutenant General Jubal Early's corps across the Potomac into Maryland, hoping to draw troops from Grant's army and break the deadlock at Petersburg. Striking east on the roads to Washington and Baltimore, Early's 15,000 men encountered a force half that size under Major General Lew Wallace. Confederate Major General John B. Gordon's division forded the Monocacy River and passed over the slope of Brooks Hill (center), only to fall back under blistering volleys from Federal troops near the Thomas House (lower right).

THE THOMAS HOUSE, "ARABY," Monocacy. All day, fighting ebbed and flowed through the fields of "Araby," the estate of Kiefer Thomas. Soldiers fired from the windows, and several shells passed through the house before Confederates finally secured it late in the day. Early had hoped to brush Wallace's force aside and move quickly on Washington, but with a division of veteran 6th Corps troops, hastily sent north from Grant's army, Wallace bought time for the capital to be reinforced. Though Wallace lost the battle, Grant said he contributed "a greater benefit to the cause than often falls to the lot of a commander by means of a victory."

MAJOR GENERAL PHILIP HENRY SHERIDAN, U.S.A., with cavalry generals. Seeking to stop the supply of food and matériel to Lee at Richmond, Grant commanded his most aggressive subordinate, Philip Sheridan (seated on ground, right), to clear Jubal Early's forces from the Shenandoah Valley. In August 1864, Sheridan organized the Army of the Shenandoah and embarked on his merciless campaign, saying, "The people must be left nothing, but their eyes to weep with over the war."

BLUE RIDGE MOUNTAINS AND SHENANDOAH VALLEY, Virginia. Sheridan brought 48,000 men to the Valley, more than twice Early's force. After a shaky start, Sheridan began to exert his numerical advantage, striking relentless blows that won victories at Winchester and Fisher's Hill. The deciding clash of the campaign came on October 19 at Cedar Creek. Sheridan was in Winchester when Early attacked at dawn and routed the Yankee troops. But "Little Phil" rode back by afternoon, rallied his beaten force, and inflicted a crushing defeat on Early. Sheridan's men won four battles in 30 days, destroyed crops, barns, mills, and farm implements, and confiscated thousands of sheep and cattle.

THE CRATER, Petersburg. In late June of 1864, Lieutenant Colonel Henry Pleasants of the 48th Pennsylvania won approval for a scheme to breach the defenses at Petersburg. A former mining engineer whose regiment included many coal miners, Pleasants supervised the excavation of a 500-foot-long tunnel from the Union works to a heavily fortified Confederate salient. His sappers stuffed 320 kegs of gunpowder in lateral galleys branching out from the end of the tunnel. At 4:44 A.M. on July 30, two volunteers crawled into the tunnel and touched off the mine, obliterating two South Carolina regiments and an artillery battery. When the debris settled, troops of Burnside's 9th Corps charged.

MAHONE MONUMENT AND THE CRATER, Petersburg. Burnside chose the 4,300 United States Colored Troops of Brigadier General Edward Ferrero's division to lead the Union assault past the Crater and onto the heights overlooking Petersburg. But at the last minute, Meade overruled him, and the lead went to a white division commanded by Brigadier General James H. Ledlie. Rather than bypassing the Crater, Ledlie's men crowded into the gaping pit, as did most of the black soldiers when they advanced in support. Confederate Major General William Mahone's counterattack overwhelmed the trapped Yankees, and Pleasants's plan ended in humiliation.

GENERAL ADELBERT AMES, U.S.A. A member of the West
Point class of May 1861 with Rosser, Upton, and Pelham,
Adelbert Ames distinguished himself in nearly every major
battle of the war. He played a vital role in the campaign against
Fort Fisher, a formidable bastion at the mouth of the Cape Fear
River. The fort protected Wilmington, North Carolina, the
South's last open port, and allowed blockade runners to
continue supplying Lee's armies. Its capture, said Secretary of
the Navy Gideon Welles, "would be almost as important as the
capture of Richmond on the fate of the Rebels."

*Under the heaviest fire, when men and officers were being stricken
down around him, he would sit on his horse, apparently unmoved
by singing rifle-ball, shrieking shot, or bursting shell, and quietly
give his orders, which were invariably communicated in the most
polite way, and generally in the form of a request. I often thought
when I saw him under fire that if one of his legs had been carried
away by a round shot he would merely turn to some officer or soldier
nearby and quietly say, "Will you kindly assist me from my horse!"*

Colonel Henry C. Lockwood, U.S.A
on General Adelbert Ames, U.S.A.
Fort Fisher

SEA FACE, Fort Fisher, North Carolina. Fort Fisher was one of the largest earthen fortifications ever constructed, a mile long on the shore and half that landward. A massive bombardment on December 24 and 25, 1864, failed to make much impression on the fort's 25-foot-thick log, sand, and sod walls or to disable more than a few of the 47 cannon. In January 1865, Grant dispatched a combined army and navy expedition, including 8,000 Union troops commanded by Major General Alfred H. Terry, to take the fort at all costs.

NORTHWEST SALIENT, Fort Fisher. Throughout January 13 and 14, Admiral David Porter's fleet rained shells on the fort, particularly the land face, where General Terry's infantry was to attack. This time, Porter's fire severely damaged the defenses. By the afternoon of January 15, 2,000 sailors and marines had landed near the sea face. The Rebels repulsed their assault, but could not restrain the simultaneous infantry charge on the northwest salient. Soon a fierce hand-to-hand battle raged down the traverses that shielded the garrison's gun emplacements.

SOUTH FROM NORTHWEST SALIENT, Fort Fisher. Colonel William Lamb, the young commander of Fort Fisher's 1,500-man garrison, struggled to stop the Yankee assailants, even ordering wounded from the fort's hospital back into the fray. But despite the devastating musketry and canister shot, the Federals continued to pour over the walls with fixed bayonets. Lamb was severely wounded, as was Major General W. H. C. Whiting, the district commander. At 10 P.M., the surviving Confederates surrendered.

HIGH BRIDGE, near Farmville, Virginia. Union troops finally breached Petersburg's defenses on April 2, 1865. That night, Lee evacuated the city, taking the Army of Northern Virginia on a desperate march west, hoping somehow to link up with Johnston's Army of Tennessee. For a week, Grant's forces pursued them, confident that the war was almost won. On the night of April 6-7, two of Lee's most trusted generals in the final campaign, William Mahone and John Gordon, led their men across the High Bridge, a 100-foot-high span that carried the South Side Railroad over the Appomattox River. Although they set fire to the bridge behind them, only a short portion was destroyed; Union pioneers doused the flames while the 2nd Corps crossed on a wagon bridge below.

HILLSMAN HOUSE, Sayler's Creek Battlefield Park, Virginia. On April 6, Sheridan's cavalry and the 6th Corps trapped more than a third of Lee's remaining forces. Union batteries on the Hillsman farm pounded General Richard Ewell's corps as the Federal infantry crossed Sayler's Creek and stormed the Rebel position. The Confederates were soon flanked and broken. Meanwhile, one mile to the south, Richard Anderson's division collapsed before charging Yankee horsemen. Three days later, Lee met Grant at Appomattox Court House to discuss the surrender of his once-invincible Army of Northern Virginia. Though other armies fought on for weeks, the war effectively ended when its two main antagonists made peace across a small table in the McLean House parlor.

APPOMATTOX COURT HOUSE NATIONAL HISTORICAL PARK, Virginia

*T*he charges were now withdrawn from the guns, the camp-fires were left to smolder in their ashes, the flags were tenderly furled—those historic banners, battle-stained, bullet-riddled, many of them but remains of their former selves, with scarcely enough left of them on which to imprint the names of the battles they had seen,—and the Army of the Union and the Army of Northern Virginia turned their backs upon each other for the first time in four long, bloody years.

Lieutenant Colonel Horace Porter, U.S.A.
Appomattox

ETERNAL LIGHT PEACE MEMORIAL, Gettysburg

Quotation Sources and Permissions
Page 15 from "When Lilacs Last in the Dooryard Bloom'd" by Walt Whitman in DRUM TAPS, 1865. Page 19 from "The Battle of Bull Run" by P. G. T. Beauregard in *The Century Magazine* 29:1 (November 1884). Page 27 from "The Capture of Fort Donelson" by Lew Wallace in *The Century Magazine* 29:2 (December 1884). Pages 28 and 127 from PERSONAL MEMOIRS OF U. S. GRANT. New York: Charles S. Webster and Co., 1885. Page 32 from "Reminiscences of War Incidents" by Capt. H. J. Cheney in *Confederate Veteran* 18:11 (November 1910). Reprinted by permission. Pages 38 and 44 from DESTRUCTION AND RECONSTRUCTION: PERSONAL EXPERIENCES OF THE LATE WAR by Richard Taylor. New York: D. Appleton and Co., 1879. Page 41 from THE WAR OF THE REBELLION: A COMPILATION OF THE OFFICIAL RECORDS OF THE UNION AND CONFEDERATE ARMIES. Washington, D.C.: Government Printing Office, 1884. Page 48 from LETTERS FROM THE PENINSULA: THE CIVIL WAR LETTERS OF GENERAL PHILIP KEARNY edited by William B. Styple. Kearny, New Jersey: Belle Grove Publishing Co., 1988. Reprinted by permission. Page 52 from "Our March Against Pope" by James Longstreet in BATTLES AND LEADERS OF THE CIVIL WAR, Vol. 2. New York: The Century Co., 1887. Page 54 from FROM MANASSAS TO APPOMATTOX by James Longstreet. Philadelphia: J.B. Lippincott Co., 1895. Page 57 from DAYS AND EVENTS by Thomas L. Livermore. Boston and New York: Houghton Mifflin Co., The Riverside Press, 1920. Reprinted by permission. Page 62 from THE ANTIETAM AND FREDERICKSBURG by Francis William Palfrey. New York: Charles Scribner's Sons, 1882. Page 68 from "Bragg's Invasion of Kentucky" by C. C. Gilbert in *Southern Bivouac* 1:9 (February 1886). Page 78 from COLONEL JOHN PELHAM: LEE'S BOY ARTILLERIST by William Woods Hassler. Richmond, Virginia: Garrett & Massie, Inc., 1960. Page 82 from MEMOIRS OF ROBERT E. LEE edited by A. L. Long and Marcus J. Wright. New York and Philadelphia:

J. M. Stoddart & Co., 1886. Pages 84 and 102 from THE LIFE AND LETTERS OF GEORGE GORDON MEADE edited by George G. Meade, Jr. New York: Charles Scribner's Sons, 1913. Reprinted by permission. Page 88 from WEARING OF THE GRAY by John Esten Cooke. New York: E. B. Treat & Co., 1867. Page 91 from CAMP FIRES OF THE CONFEDERACY by Ben L. LeBree. Louisville, Kentucky: Courier Journal Job Printing Co., 1899. Page 99 from LIFE AND LETTERS OF ALEXANDER HAYS edited by George Thornton Fleming. Pittsburgh, Pennsylvania, 1919. Page 110 from CHICKAMAUGA: BLOODY BATTLE IN THE WILDERNESS by Glenn Tucker. Indianapolis and New York: The Bobbs-Merrill Co., 1961. Copyright © 1961 by the Bobbs-Merrill Company, Inc. Reprinted with permission of Macmillan Publishing Company. Page 117 from "The Grand Strategy of the War of the Rebellion" by William T. Sherman in *The Century Magazine* 35:4 (February 1888). Page 118 from THE COMMANCHES by Frank M. Myers, introduction by Lee Wallace. Gaithersburg, Maryland: Butternut Press, Inc., 1987. Reprinted by permission of Ron Van Sickle. Page 120 from THE LIFE AND LETTERS OF EMORY UPTON. New York: Appleton and Co., 1885. Page 136 from "A Man from Maine" by Henry C. Lockwood in the *Maine Bugle* 1:1 (January 1894). Page 143 from "Grant's Last Campaign" by Horace Porter in *The Century Magazine* 35:1 (November 1887).

Archival Photography Credits
Pages 2, 20, 28, 48, 52, 58, 70, 73, 85, 94, 96, 102, 108, 112, 120, 123, 124, and 132 from the Massachusetts Commandery, Miltary Order of the Loyal Legion and the U.S. Army Military History Institute, Carlisle, Pennsylvania. Page 6 from the U.S. Army Military History Institute. Page 7 from the Alderman Library, University of Virginia, Charlottesville, Virginia. Pages 32, 42, 128, and 136 from the Library of Congress, Washington, D.C. Pages 38, 54, 68, 78, 88, 118, and 134 from the Valentine Museum, Richmond, Virginia. Page 44 from the Virginia Historical Society, Richmond, Virginia.